COLDPLAY   X&Y

ISBN 1-4234-0231-6

HAL•LEONARD®
CORPORATION
7777 W. BLUEMOUND RD. P.O. BOX 13819 MILWAUKEE, WI 53213

Visit Hal Leonard Online at
www.halleonard.com

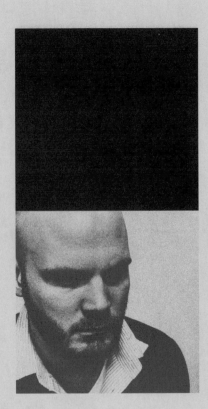

Management by Estelle Wilkinson and Dave Holmes.

Music arrangements by Derek Jones.
Music processed by Paul Ewers Music Design.
Edited by Lucy Holliday.
Original Design and Art Direction: Tappin Gofton.
Photography: Kevin Westenberg, Tom Sheehan and Coldplay.

SQUARE ONE

Words & Music by Guy Berryman, Jon Buckland, Will Champion & Chris Martin

The fu - ture's_ for dis - co - ver - ing___ the

space in which we're tra - vel - ling.

From the top___ of the first page___
The first line of the first page___

I need a com - pass, draw me a map.

I'm on the top, I can't get back.

D.S. al Coda

(Oh,_____ oh.)_____

WHAT IF

Words & Music by Guy Berryman, Jon Buckland, Will Champion & Chris Martin

that you don't___ want___ me there___ by___ your side,___ that you don't___

___ want___ me there in___ your life?___

2. What if I___ got it wrong_____ and no po - em___ or
3. Ev -'ry step___ that you take_____ could be your big - gest mis -

song_____ could put right___ what I got wrong_____
-take._____ It could bend___ or it could break_____

or make you feel__ I be - long?_____
that's the risk__ that you take._____

And what if you__ should de - cide_____ that you don't__ want__ me there by__ your side,__
2° in your life,__

that you don't__ want__ me there in__ your life?__
2° by your side?__

Ooh,_____ that's right,_____

20

let's take a breath, jump ov - er the side._____

Ooh,_____ that's right,_____

how can you know it if you don't ev - en try?_____

2° when
(they say) you know that dark - ness al - ways turns in - to light._____

1.
Ooh,_____ that's right._____

2.
Ooh,_____ that's

21

22

WHITE SHADOWS

Words & Music by Guy Berryman, Jon Buckland, Will Champion & Chris Martin

24

27

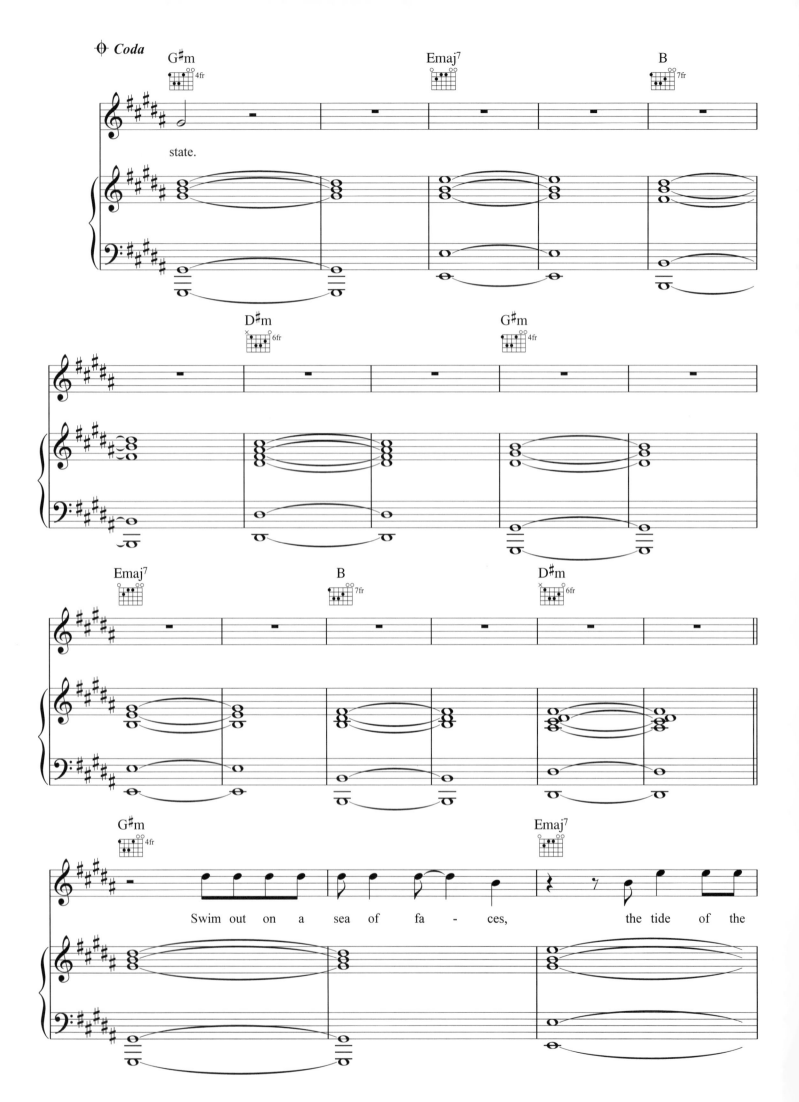

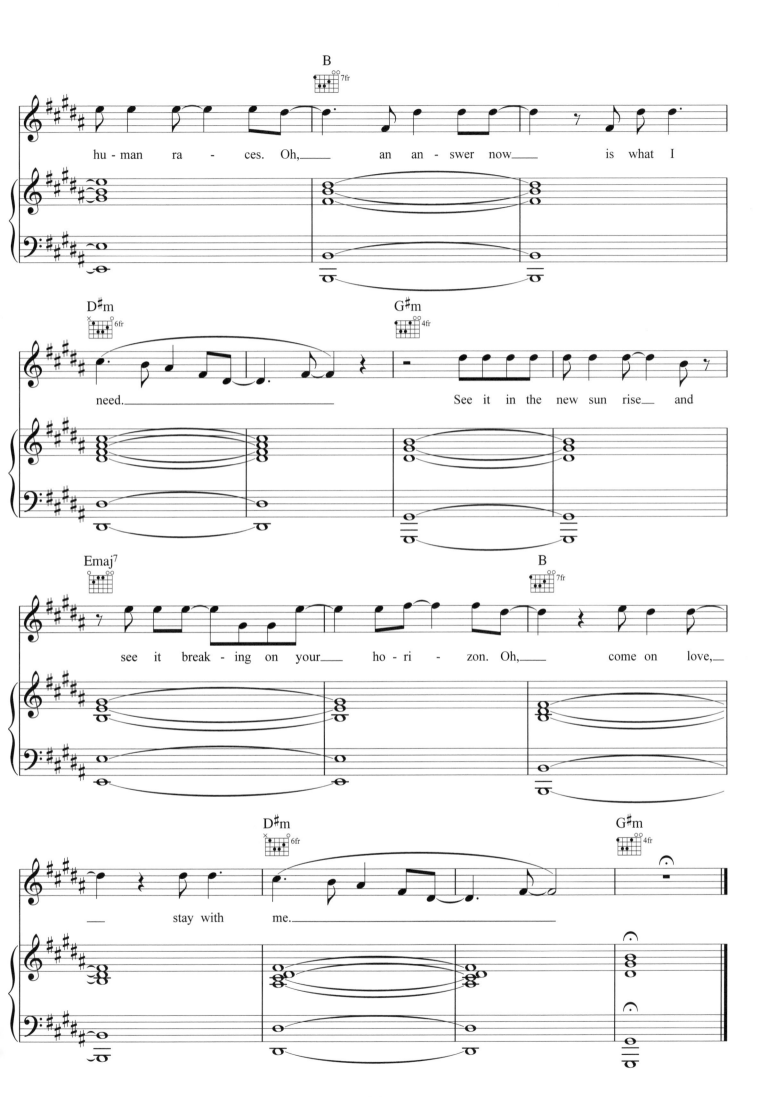

FIX YOU

Words & Music by Guy Berryman, Jon Buckland, Will Champion & Chris Martin

Lights will guide you home and ig - nite your bones

and I will try to fix you.

3. And

Guitar

Tears stream__ down your face__

when you lose some-thing you can-not re - place.__

TALK

Words & Music by Guy Berryman, Jon Buckland, Will Champion,
Chris Martin, Karl Bartos, Ralf Huetter & Emil Schult

to talk to you.

You could take a pic - ture of
(3°) don't know where you're go-ing and you

some-thing you see.
want to talk.

In the fu - ture where will I be?
feel like you're go-ing where you've been be - fore.

You

And they're talk - ing it___ to me.___

So you

D.S. al Coda

Coda I

some - thing that's nev - er been done.___ Do___

some-thing that's nev - er been done.___

43

X&Y

Words & Music by Guy Berryman, Jon Buckland, Will Champion & Chris Martin

and sing- ing_____ ooh._____

Ooh._____

Ooh.

Ooh.

Repeat to fade

49

SPEED OF SOUND

Words & Music by Guy Berryman, Jon Buckland, Will Champion & Chris Martin

1. How long be-fore I get in, be-fore it
2. Look up, I look up at night, pla-nets are mov-
3. I-deas that you'll ne-ver find, all the in-ven-

54

A MESSAGE

Words & Music by Guy Berryman, Jon Buckland, Will Champion & Chris Martin

58

song_____ is love,___ is love_____ un - known___ and I've got_ to get___ that mes - sage_____ home.___

LOW

Words & Music by Guy Berryman, Jon Buckland, Will Champion & Chris Martin

THE HARDEST PART

Words & Music by Guy Berryman, Jon Buckland, Will Champion & Chris Martin

I could feel___ it___ go down.___
I could feel___ it___ go down.___

Bit - ter - sweet___ I___ could taste___
You left the sweet - est___ taste__

___ in my mouth.___ Sil - ver lin -
___ in my mouth.___ Sil - ver lin -

- ing___ the clouds.___ Oh, and I,___
- ing___ the cloud.___ Oh, and I,___

wish that I could work it out.___

Oh, and I,___

I won-der what it's all a -bout.____

Con pedale

won-der what it's all a -bout.____

I

74

SWALLOWED IN THE SEA

Words & Music by Guy Berryman, Jon Buckland, Will Champion & Chris Martin

TWISTED LOGIC

Words & Music by Guy Berryman, Jon Buckland, Will Champion & Chris Martin

first time   ri - vers will run.

2. Hun - dreds   of years in the fu - ture
(3.) - at - ed,   then drilled and in - va - ded.

You'll go back-wards_____ but then you'll go.__

Guitar

3. Cre -

D.S. al Coda

𝄋 *Coda*

TIL KINGDOM COME

Words & Music by Guy Berryman, Jon Buckland, Will Champion & Chris Martin

ing, the drum-mer be-gins to drum.___ I don't

know which way___ I'm go - ing. I don't know which way___ I've come.___

2. Hold my
3. In your

92

95

123456789